Creatures of the Sea

Books by John Christopher Fine

SUNKEN SHIPS AND TREASURE
OCEANS IN PERIL
THE HUNGER ROAD

Creatures of the Sea

Text and photographs by
JOHN CHRISTOPHER FINE

ATHENEUM   **1989**   **NEW YORK**

Atheneum
Macmillan Publishing Company
866 Third Avenue, New York, NY 10022
Collier Macmillan Canada, Inc.
First Edition
Printed in Singapore

10 9 8 7 6 5 4 3 2 1

Library of Congress Cataloging-in-Publication Data
Fine, John Christopher.
Creatures of the sea /
text and photographs by John Christopher Fine
—1st ed.   p.   cm.
Summary: Describes sea creatures with unusual appearances or
behaviors that allow them to fit successfully into their underwater
environment.
ISBN 0-689-31420-5
1. Marine fauna—Juvenile literature.   [1. Marine animals.
2. Camouflage (Biology)   3. Animal defenses.]   I. Title.
QL122.2.F56   1989
591.92—dc19
89-34   CIP   AC

INTRODUCTION

All creatures have senses, instincts, and ways of behaving to survive in the wild. The strange-looking fish that buries itself in the sand, the animal that has funny-looking fringes or bumps over its body to make it look like its home, and the quick-change artists, switching colors to blend in with the background—all have a purpose in nature. Their odd colors, shapes, and disguises help to keep them from being eaten by larger animals or to attract the opposite sex.

Animals acquire their odd behavior and funny looks because over a long period of time these help them survive. Sometimes when animals reproduce, it happens that some offspring are born that are different from the rest. If this difference gives the creature an advantage in nature, if it can hide better to escape being eaten or swim faster to catch more food, then that animal may survive to reproduce and have offspring of its own. The offspring born from this "different" individual are likely to have the "new" advantage that helps them survive better wherever they live.

When we humans observe oddly colored and shaped animals that behave in ways that are strange to us, we think they are funny. We may even say that these creatures look crazy or are being silly on purpose. Animals in the sea are no exception. They are born, live, reproduce, and sometimes along the way they make people laugh.

Come along as our candid camera captures some of these sea creatures at home in the ocean and discover how and why they behave the way they do, to fit into their underwater environment.

HERMIT CRAB

These little creatures live in discarded shells. When a hermit crab finds a shell that fits, it lives in it until it grows too big, then it looks for a larger home. Sometimes the shell attracts a hitchhiker, like the anemone on the right, which has taken up residence on top of the hermit crab's shell home. The adult anemone can't move on its own, so it depends on the crab to carry it from place to place.

FILEFISH

Filefish have the ability to change colors quickly to hide from enemies. These fast-change artists can remain perfectly still, almost invisible, against coral.

TRUMPET FISH

Trumpet fish also can change colors to enable them to remain hidden among coral. This long, needlelike fish was given its name because of its trumpet-shaped mouth.

CONE SHELL

The creature that lives in the cone shell has a poisonous dart. The dart can release a deadly venom into its prey, usually worms or small fish. Once a cone-shell animal has darted its prey to death, it sets about eating it. Shell collectors handle live cone shells by the thick end to avoid their venomous sting. Cone shells are found in tropical seas. The rarest and most beautiful specimens live in the Pacific Ocean.

LIMA CLAM

The Lima clam propels itself along the sea bottom by clapping its shell together. It extends its tentacles to bring it its food. The Lima clam pictured here was photographed in the Caribbean Sea. Some other species of bivalves, or two-shelled creatures, such as scallops and mussels, live in colder waters and are gathered for food.

ANGLERFISH

The anglerfish, or lotte, resembles the bottom of the sea, where it hides. It remains perfectly still, extending the long wand that is attached to its head. This "fishing pole" has a fleshy "lure" at the end. To other fish this lure looks like food, and when they draw near to eat it, the anglerfish springs up and eats them. So, anglerfish actually fish for their food.

FLOUNDER

Can you see it? This little flounder, or sole, is buried in the sand. Because it can change color by means of special cells in its skin, the flounder is able to hide from predators that would eat it. This is also an effective disguise when the flounder is hunting other fish for food.

CRINOIDS

Marine crinoids, the sea lily and feather star, are actually animals, although they look like plants with long branches. The crinoid attaches itself to coral or large basket sponges. At night it extends long arms to feed. During the daytime or when it is disturbed the crinoid can pull itself into a small ball. The crinoid has "legs" it can use to attach itself to a branch of coral or sponge. It also uses these legs to move about.

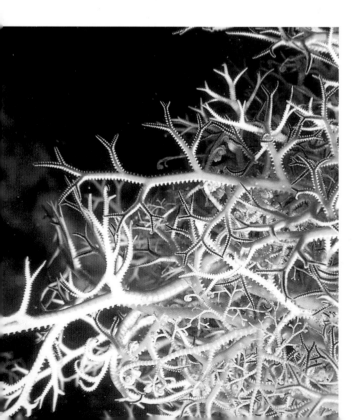

CHRISTMAS TREE WORM

Christmas tree worms, or serpulids, also live attached to coral and extend their delicate spirals to feed. When they detect danger, they withdraw quickly into their calcium home.

NUDIBRANCH

The nudibranch gets its name from two words that
mean naked gills. These tiny and colorful creatures
are really sea slugs, like snails without the hard outside
protection. Nudibranchs eat things that make them
very bad tasting. Once a fish has tried a nibble of one,
it never tries again. Their funny shapes and bright
colors are their best protection because they are
quickly recognized by hungry fish. The delicate lacelike
structures are actually gills that allow nudibranchs to
breathe underwater.

PUFFER FISH

Puffer fish gulp water to expand into large balls, some the size of basketballs. Some have sharp spines that stick out when they puff up, discouraging large fish from swallowing them. In some places in the world, the puffer fish is a prized delicacy, although it must be prepared by experts, since some parts of the fish are extremely poisonous.

BRISTLE WORM

Bristle worms look like underwater caterpillars crawling along the bottom of the sea. The tufts on their bodies are actually stingers that can give a painful wound. Sometimes divers touch the bristles with the tip of a snorkle just to watch the worm puff up in defense. Bristle worms can often be seen eating dead fish or jellyfish on the ocean floor or grazing on coral polyps.

CORAL

Corals are colonial animals. That means they live together in groups or colonies. There are soft and hard corals, but in any form, a coral is an animal, not a plant, and begins life as a free swimming larva. Corals are mighty builders in tropical seas and oceans, forming huge underwater mountains, called reefs. New corals grow on top of old, and some coral reefs may be millions of years old. Brightly colored polyps, the coral animal, extend from their home in the reef at night to feed, drawing minute plant and animal matter into their mouth parts.

Coral reefs are formed in warm, clear water where the temperature seldom drops below sixty-eight degrees Fahrenheit. While there are some species of cold-water corals, these varieties are not reef builders.

CROCODILE FISH

The crocodile fish, or platypus fish, is long and thin, with a flat face. It lies almost invisible on the bottom of the ocean, waiting for prey to happen near. With a thrust of its powerful tail, it swims up and catches the food in its mouth.

STONEFISH

Stonefish are almost invisible on the bottom of the ocean because they look like stones or rocks. In fact, it really takes a keen eye to spot the fish in these pictures unless you know it is there. Sharp dorsal spines, or needlelike darts on the stonefish's back, contain a deadly venom, and some stonefish from the Coral Sea have caused fatal wounds when swimmers have accidentally stepped on them while wading. Like many of the other creatures in this book, stonefish simply lie in wait for dinner. When unsuspecting prey happens near, the stonefish swims up fast and gulps it down.

CLOWN FISH

The clown fish gets its name from its bright orange or red color and the stripes or bands on its body. These little fish live together with sea anemones. The anemones' tentacles have stinging cells that can kill fish that happen to swim near. The anemone cannot move from place to place, so its tentacles catch food and bring it to its oral cavity, or "mouth." Scientists believe that clown fish have developed a film on their skin that prevents the anemone from stinging them. Clown fish

act as lures or decoys, attracting other fish into range of the stinging tentacles of the anemone. As a reward, the clown fish get protection and can eat part of what the anemone has been able to catch.

MORAY EEL

The moray eel looks fearsome underwater. They continually open and close their mouths, exposing long fangs. This looks scary, but it actually is done to help the animal push water over its gills to breathe. Although its teeth are dangerous, the moray, like most creatures in nature, usually only attacks in order to capture food to eat. Morays can grow to eight feet or more in length and are often found in caves, in coral or in shipwrecks, venturing out at night to hunt.

LIONFISH

With its spines extended, the *Pterois*, or lionfish, is
ready to defend itself. This is another fish whose spines
contain venom and can give a nasty sting.

BATFISH

The batfish resting on the ocean bottom looks like a piece of rock or coral. When the batfish spots prey, it springs up and swallows it. The unsuspecting dinner thought the batfish was part of the scenery.

BOXFISH

The boxfish's hard body and small fins give it an odd appearance. It seems to hover in the water like a tiny helicopter. Juvenile boxfish look like small marbles with polka dots. As the boxfish matures it develops patches on its skin to add to its unusual looks.

TURKEY FISH and SCORPION FISH

The turkey fish, which looks like a pretty feather duster, is actually deadly. Each one of the featherlike spines on either side and the spines along its back contain a poison that can seriously injure a diver or fisherman who catches it. A relative of the turkey fish is the

scorpion fish, which also has poisonous spines on its back. Sometimes bathers in the tropics accidentally step on one of these fish, causing the venom to be injected. While stings from the scorpion fish are rarely fatal, they are very painful. These fish lie on the bottom of the sea without moving until small fish come within range. They are capable of quick bursts of speed to capture their food.

INDEX